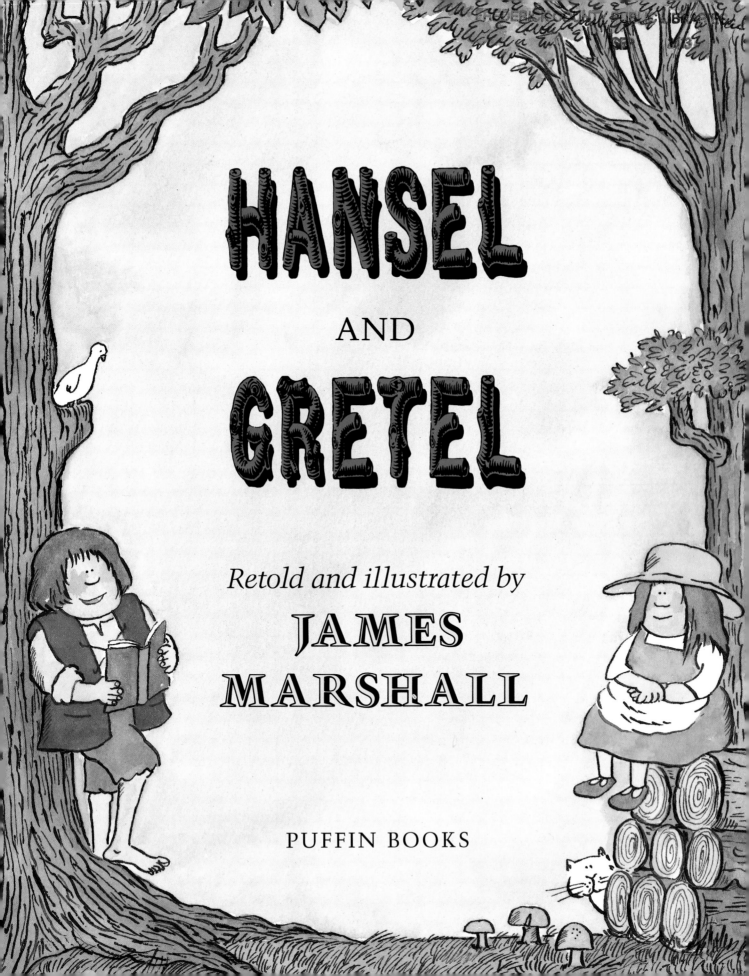

HANSEL
AND
GRETEL

Retold and illustrated by

JAMES
MARSHALL

PUFFIN BOOKS

PUFFIN BOOKS
Published by the Penguin Group
Penguin Putnam Books for Young Readers,
345 Hudson Street, New York, New York 10014, U.S.A.
Penguin Books Ltd, 27 Wrights Lane, London W8 5TZ, England
Penguin Books Australia Ltd, Ringwood, Victoria, Australia
Penguin Books Canada Ltd, 10 Alcorn Avenue, Toronto, Ontario, Canada M4V 3B2
Penguin Books (N.Z.) Ltd, 182-190 Wairau Road, Auckland 10, New Zealand
Penguin Books Ltd, Registered Offices: Harmondsworth, Middlesex, England

Originally published in hardcover by
Dial Books for Young Readers
A Division of Penguin Books USA Inc.

Library of Congress Catalog Card Number: 89-26011
Manufactured in China by South China Printing Company Limited
First Puffin Pied Piper Printing 1994
ISBN 978-0-14-050836-9

A Pied Piper Book is a registered trademark of
Dial Books for Young Readers,
A Division of Penguin Books USA Inc.,
® TM 1,163,686 and ® TM 1,054,312.

31 32 33 34 35 36 37 38 39 40

HANSEL AND GRETEL
is also published in hardcover editions by
Dial Books for Young Readers.

To Laurie Sale

• • •

Once upon a time
in a cottage near a vast forest
there lived a poor woodcutter,
his wife, and his two children.
The boy was called Hansel,
and the girl Gretel.

At the best of times
the family had precious little to live on.
But now there was a great famine in the land,
and food was scarcer than ever.
The woodcutter's wife was worried
there wouldn't be enough for her.
"Those wretched children of yours
are gobbling everything up!" she said to her husband.
"Do you want your pretty little wife to waste away?
Something will have to be done."
"Yes, my dearest," said the poor woodcutter,
who was afraid of his wife's ferocious temper.
"She doesn't like us," said Gretel.
"Yes she does," said Hansel.
But he didn't mean it.

One night when the woodcutter was tossing and turning
and worrying about how to feed his family,
his wife revealed a plan.
"Listen to this," she whispered in her husband's ear.
"We will take the children into the woods,
give them a bit of bread, and leave them there."
"Never!" cried the woodcutter.
But his wife badgered and badgered.

"My poor children!" cried the woodcutter.

"I know what's best, you dolt!" said his wife.

"Oh dear," whispered Gretel.

"Don't worry," said Hansel, "I'll take care of us."

And slipping out into the moonlit night, he gathered up
as many white pebbles as he could find.

"What are you doing?" said Gretel.

"You'll see," said Hansel.

"Up, you lazybones!" cried the woodcutter's wife
early the next morning.
"It's time to go to the forest to fetch wood."
And she gave Hansel and Gretel a crust of bread.
"Save it for lunch; it's all you'll get."
The family set off.
In a short while Hansel stopped and turned around.
Soon he did it again.
"Why are you lagging behind, Hansel?" asked his father.

"I'm looking back at my white kitten
on the roof," said Hansel.
"You donkey!" snapped the woodcutter's wife.
"That's not your kitten,
that's the morning sun on the chimney."
They entered the vast forest.

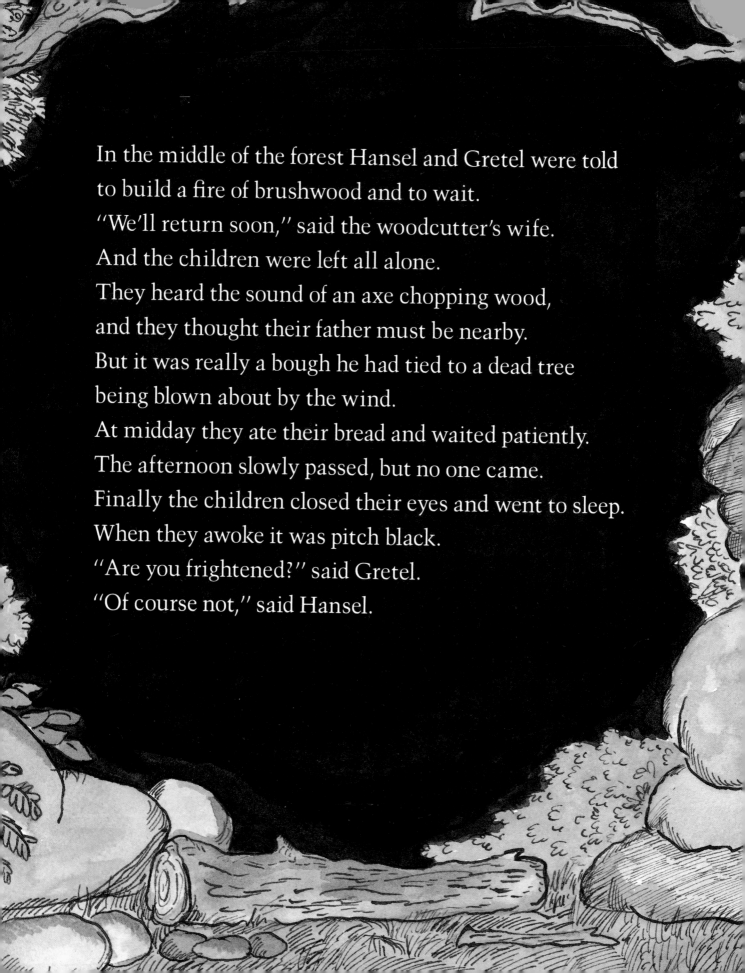

In the middle of the forest Hansel and Gretel were told
to build a fire of brushwood and to wait.
"We'll return soon," said the woodcutter's wife.
And the children were left all alone.
They heard the sound of an axe chopping wood,
and they thought their father must be nearby.
But it was really a bough he had tied to a dead tree
being blown about by the wind.
At midday they ate their bread and waited patiently.
The afternoon slowly passed, but no one came.
Finally the children closed their eyes and went to sleep.
When they awoke it was pitch black.
"Are you frightened?" said Gretel.
"Of course not," said Hansel.

When the moon had risen, Hansel took Gretel
by the hand and showed her how they could follow
the trail of white pebbles.
"What a clever brother I have!" said Gretel.
It took them the rest of the night to get out of the forest.

When the children arrived home at daybreak,
the woodcutter's wife was shocked and infuriated,
although she quickly pretended to be glad to see them.
"We thought you were *never* coming back!" she said.

Hansel and Gretel believed the worst to be over.

But soon there came another famine,

and the woodcutter's wife began to fret.

"There's hardly enough for the two of us to eat,"

she said to her husband.

"We'll simply have to take the children back to the woods."

"Not again," whispered Gretel.

"Don't worry," said Hansel.

But when he went to gather up more pebbles,

he found the door bolted—*she* had seen to that.

The next morning the children were given a bit of bread,

and the family set off.

Every few paces Hansel turned around to strew

a handful of breadcrumbs behind him.

"Why are you tarrying, Hansel?" said his father.

"I'm looking back at my white pigeon on the roof,"

said Hansel.

"Simpleton!" cried the woodcutter's wife.

"That isn't your pigeon,

that's the morning sun on the chimney."

When they came to the most forbidding part of the forest,
the woodcutter's wife said, "You will wait here
while your father and I gather wood. We will be back soon."
Hansel and Gretel did not believe her.
At midday Gretel shared her bread with Hansel.
Soon, as they did before, they fell asleep.
And when they awoke, it was pitch black.
"Oooh," said Gretel.
"When the moon rises," said Hansel, "we will follow
the trail of breadcrumbs out of the woods."
But when the moon rose, they found no breadcrumbs.
The birds in the forest had eaten them all.
"We'll never get out!" cried Gretel.
They wandered on, deeper and deeper into the forest,
eating whatever berries they could find.
When they'd been away from home for three days,
a snow-white bird appeared.
"Let's follow it," said Hansel.

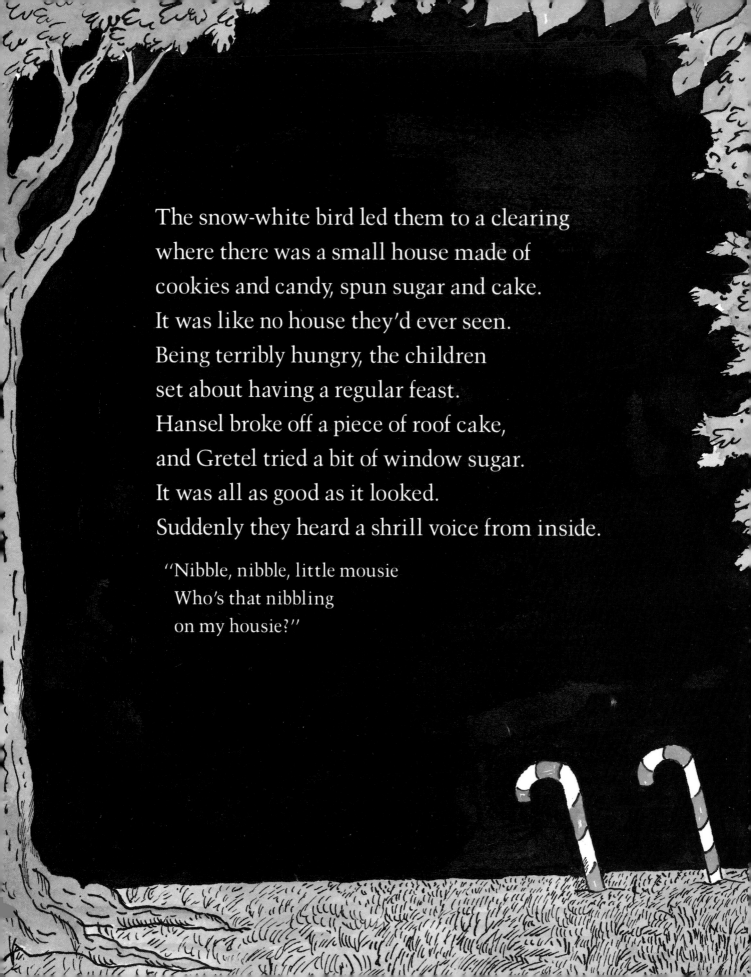

The snow-white bird led them to a clearing
where there was a small house made of
cookies and candy, spun sugar and cake.
It was like no house they'd ever seen.
Being terribly hungry, the children
set about having a regular feast.
Hansel broke off a piece of roof cake,
and Gretel tried a bit of window sugar.
It was all as good as it looked.
Suddenly they heard a shrill voice from inside.

"Nibble, nibble, little mousie
  Who's that nibbling
  on my housie?"

The door flew open.

"What's this?" said a lady, who Gretel was *sure*

was a witch.

"Two tasty—uh—pretty children have come to stay.

Now don't be alarmed, my angels.

I'm really *very* sweet."

And she took Hansel and Gretel by the hand

and led them inside, where a sumptuous dinner

of sugared pancakes with apples and nuts had been prepared.

Hansel and Gretel ate until they were perfectly stuffed.

"Time for sleep now," said the lady.

And she tucked them into snug warm beds

and tiptoed away.

"She's nice," said Hansel.

"Hmmm," said Gretel.

The next morning the lady, who was *indeed* a witch,
snatched Hansel from his bed, carried him outside,
and tossed him right into a cage.
"Lovely!" said the witch. "Lovely!
This is where I shall fatten you up.
And when you're all plump and juicy,
I shall have a regular feast!"
"You let my brother out!" cried Gretel.
But the witch, who was delighted with her handiwork,
only cackled and did a little dance.

Poor Gretel, who had to do the witch's bidding,
was put to work cooking enormous meals for Hansel.
For her own dinner, Gretel was given only crab shells.
Every morning the witch would go to Hansel's cage
to see how much fatter he'd grown.
"Hansel, stick out your finger," she said.
And Hansel would stick out an old chicken bone.
(Witches, as everyone knows, have beady red eyes
and dreadfully bad eyesight.)
"I simply don't understand it," said the witch.
"You're as thin as a bone—can't eat you yet!"

Now Hansel's little trick worked for some time.
Every morning the hungry witch was annoyed
to find him still so scrawny.
"Phooey!" said the witch. "Not yet!"
But finally she had run completely out of patience.
"I'll just have to eat you as you are," she said.
And she had a consoling thought.
Perhaps she should eat the little one too.
"Gretel, dear," she said, "would you please peek
into the oven to see if it is sufficiently hot?"
But Gretel saw what she had in mind.
"I don't know how," she said stupidly.
"Goose!" cried the witch. "I'll show you!"
And she crawled partially into the oven.
Really, there was only one thing for Gretel to do.
She gave the witch a tremendous shove.

The horrid witch roasted to a regular crisp.
"We're free!" cried Gretel. "The witch is dead!"
Hansel flew out of the cage like a bird.
"What a clever little sister I have!" he cried.
Together they explored the witch's house,
where they found boxes and boxes
of precious gems and gold coins.

"Better than pebbles!" said Hansel.
"But now it is time to leave the witch's wood."
When they had wandered about for some time,
they came to a wide lake.
A kindly duck offered to ferry them across.
As they neared the opposite shore Gretel was sure
they could see their father's house in the distance.

When the children reached home
their father welcomed them with open arms,
for he loved them dearly
and had been miserable without them.
He told them his wife had died.
Whether Hansel and Gretel were sorry
is difficult to say.
But with their father they lived
happily ever after.